AF326512

ROY PEACOCK

The Urban Hydroponic Blueprint

Sustainable Gardening for Small Spaces

Contents

1

Understanding the Basics of Hydroponics

Hydroponics may sound like a complicated scientific process, but at its core, it's simply a method of growing plants without soil. By using water enriched with nutrients, you can provide plants with everything they need to thrive while eliminating the need for traditional gardening practices. For urban dwellers, where outdoor space is often scarce, hydroponics offers an efficient, space-saving, and eco-friendly way to grow fresh produce.

In this chapter, we'll break down the fundamental concepts of hydroponics, explore why it's ideal for beginners, and look at the six main types of hydroponic systems to help you decide which one is best for your needs.

—-

What Is Hydroponics?

The word "hydroponics" comes from the Greek words hydro (water) and ponos (labor), essentially meaning "working water." In a hydroponic system, plants are grown in nutrient-rich water solutions rather than soil. The water delivers essential minerals directly to the plant's roots, making the growing process faster and more efficient. Since plants don't need to expend energy searching for nutrients in the soil, they can focus their energy on growing stronger stems, bigger leaves, and, ultimately, higher yields.

Hydroponics isn't new. Ancient civilizations such as the Babylonians used hydroponic techniques to create the Hanging Gardens of Babylon, one of the Seven Wonders of the Ancient World. Modern hydroponics, however, has become more accessible due to advances in technology and the availability of affordable materials.

—-

Why Choose Hydroponics?

Hydroponics has several advantages, especially for urban gardeners:

1. Space-Saving: Traditional gardening requires a significant amount of space, but hydroponics systems can be compact, making them ideal for apartments, balconies, and other small urban spaces.

2. Efficiency: Plants grow faster in hydroponic systems because they receive nutrients directly and consistently. You can grow vegetables like lettuce in half the time it takes with soil.

3. Water Conservation: Surprisingly, hydroponics uses up to 90% less water than soil-based gardening. The water circulates within the system, so very little is wasted.

4. No Soil, No Mess: Since there's no soil involved, there's no weeding, and pests that thrive in dirt are less of an issue.

5. Year-Round Gardening: With a controlled indoor setup, you can grow fresh produce regardless of the season.

—-

The Six Types of Hydroponic Systems

When it comes to hydroponics, there isn't a one-size-fits-all solution. Depending on your space, budget, and goals, you can choose from six main types of systems. Here's a quick overview:

1. Wick System:

Best For: Beginners

How It Works: Nutrients are delivered to plants via a wick that draws the solution from a reservoir.

Pros: Simple and low-cost.

Cons: Limited to small plants like herbs.

2. Deep Water Culture (DWC):

Best For: Growing leafy greens like lettuce.

How It Works: Plants are suspended above a nutrient solution with their roots submerged in the water.

Pros: Low maintenance and highly efficient.

Cons: Requires oxygenation of water using an air pump.

3. Nutrient Film Technique (NFT):

Best For: Experienced hobbyists.

How It Works: A thin film of nutrient solution flows continuously over the plant roots.

Pros: Uses less water and nutrients.

Cons: Can be tricky to maintain; pumps must run constantly.

4. Ebb and Flow (Flood and Drain):

Best For: Versatile gardeners.

How It Works: The growing area is periodically flooded with nutrient solution, then drained back into the reservoir.

Pros: Supports a wide variety of plants.

Cons: Requires more setup and equipment.

5. Aeroponics:

Best For: Tech-savvy gardeners.

How It Works: Plant roots are suspended in the air and misted with nutrient solution.

Pros: Maximizes oxygen exposure for roots.

Cons: Expensive and requires precise control.

6. Kratky Method:

Best For: Minimalists.

How It Works: Plants are suspended above a stagnant nutrient solution with no need for pumps or electricity.

Pros: Inexpensive and easy to set up.

Cons: Limited to smaller plants.

—-

How to Get Started with Hydroponics

For beginners, the Kratky method or a wick system is a great place to start. These systems are simple to build, require minimal maintenance, and don't need specialized equipment like pumps or timers. With just a few household items, such as a plastic container, some nutrient solution, and plant seedlings, you can begin your hydroponic journey.

Supplies Checklist:

A container or reservoir (e.g., a plastic tote or jar)

Growing medium (e.g., perlite, coco coir, or Rockwool)

Hydroponic nutrient solution

Net pots to hold your plants

A small water pump (optional for more advanced systems)

—-

Case Study: Sarah's Journey from Apartment Balcony to Thriving Herb Garden

Sarah, a 32-year-old teacher living in a one-bedroom apartment, had always dreamed of growing her own herbs and vegetables. However, with no backyard and limited balcony space, she assumed it wasn't possible—until she discovered hydroponics.

Using the Kratky method, Sarah set up a small herb garden on her balcony. She started with a few mason jars, some basil seeds, and a pre-mixed nutrient solution. Within weeks, her basil plants were flourishing, and she soon expanded her setup to include cilantro, parsley, and even cherry tomatoes.

"Hydroponics completely changed the way I think about gardening," Sarah says. "I thought you needed a lot of space and time, but it's so easy once you get the hang of it."

—-

Hydroponics and Sustainability

Hydroponics isn't just a solution for urban living; it's also an eco-friendly way to grow food. By conserving water and eliminating the need for chemical-laden soil, hydroponic systems can significantly reduce your environmental impact. For city dwellers, hydroponics offers the opportunity to grow fresh, pesticide-free produce right at home, cutting down on the carbon footprint of store-bought vegetables.

—-

Key Takeaways

Hydroponics is a simple, efficient way to grow plants without soil.

It's ideal for urban gardeners with limited space.

There are six main types of systems, ranging from beginner-friendly to advanced.

Starting small with a DIY system like the Kratky method can help you build confidence and skills.

With hydroponics, you can enjoy fresh, homegrown produce year-round, no matter where you live.

Now that you understand the basics, let's move on to the next chapter, where we'll explore how to plan your hydroponic space to maximize efficiency and results.

2

Planning Your Hydroponic Space

Before diving into setting up your hydroponic garden, it's essential to plan your space. One of the greatest advantages of hydroponics is its flexibility—it can fit almost anywhere. Whether you live in a compact apartment, have a small balcony, or even just a sunny windowsill, hydroponics can adapt to your space. In this chapter, we'll guide you through evaluating your available space, understanding the key environmental factors for plant growth, and setting up a layout that works for your needs.

—-

Step 1: Assessing Your Space

The first step in planning your hydroponic garden is identifying where it will go. The space you choose will determine the type of hydroponic system you can use, the plants you can grow, and how you'll manage the system.

Key Considerations:

1. Size: Measure the area you're planning to use. Even a small area, such as a shelf or a corner of your kitchen, can be enough for a beginner's system.

2. Access to Light: Plants need light to grow, so consider spaces near windows or under artificial lights. South-facing windows are ideal for natural sunlight.

3. Proximity to Power and Water: Many hydroponic systems require electricity for pumps or grow lights, so ensure the space has access to an outlet. Easy access to water makes refilling your system more convenient.

4. Ventilation: Good airflow prevents mold and pests. Avoid spaces that are too enclosed or humid.

5. Temperature Control: Most plants thrive in temperatures between 65°F and 75°F (18°C–24°C). Avoid areas prone to temperature extremes, like next to a heater or drafty window.

Example Layouts:

Windowsill Garden: Ideal for herbs or small plants using the

Kratky method.

Balcony Setup: Perfect for larger plants in vertical systems or deep water culture setups.

Closet Garden: Requires grow lights and ventilation but offers complete control over the growing environment.

— -

Step 2: Lighting Your Garden

Light is the most critical factor for plant growth. In traditional gardening, sunlight provides the full spectrum of light plants need to photosynthesize. With hydroponics, especially indoors, you may need to supplement natural light with artificial grow lights.

Options for Lighting:

1. Natural Light: If your chosen space gets six or more hours of direct sunlight daily, you might not need artificial lights. However, cloudy days and seasonal changes can limit sunlight availability.

2. Grow Lights: These are designed to mimic the sunlight spectrum. Popular options include:

LED Grow Lights: Energy-efficient, long-lasting, and customizable for different plant types.

Fluorescent Lights: Affordable and suitable for small setups, but less efficient than LEDs.

High-Intensity Discharge (HID) Lights: Powerful and best for large-scale setups, but they produce heat and consume more energy.

Tips for Using Grow Lights:

Keep lights 12–18 inches above plants to prevent overheating.

Use a timer to simulate day-night cycles (e.g., 16 hours on, 8 hours off for most vegetables).

Adjust the light spectrum depending on the plant's growth stage: blue light for leafy growth and red light for flowering.

— -

Step 3: Environmental Factors

In addition to light, plants need the right environmental conditions to thrive. Here's what to consider:

1. Airflow and Humidity:

Plants need fresh air for photosynthesis and to prevent mold and mildew.

Use a small fan to keep air circulating in enclosed spaces.

Maintain humidity levels between 40%–70%, depending on the plant type.

2. Temperature:

Most plants prefer consistent temperatures. Use a thermometer to monitor the growing area.

For cooler spaces, consider a heating mat under your system. For hot areas, use shade cloth or ventilation.

3. Space for Growth:

Ensure each plant has enough room for its roots and foliage. Crowding plants can lead to competition for nutrients and reduced yields.

—-

Step 4: Choosing the Right Setup for Your Space

Based on your space assessment, you can now decide on the best hydroponic system and layout. Here are a few ideas tailored to different spaces:

Small Spaces (e.g., apartments or windowsills):

System: Kratky method or wick system.

Plants: Herbs, lettuce, or microgreens.

Example Setup: Mason jars or small containers on a windowsill.

Medium Spaces (e.g., balconies or kitchens):

System: Deep water culture (DWC) or ebb and flow.

Plants: Spinach, peppers, or strawberries.

Example Setup: A storage bin system with an air pump.

Large Spaces (e.g., spare rooms or garages):

System: Vertical garden or nutrient film technique (NFT).

Plants: Tomatoes, cucumbers, or larger fruiting plants.

Example Setup: Shelving units with grow lights and nutrient solution reservoirs.

— -

Case Study: How John Converted His Closet into a Lush Vegetable Garden

John, a college student living in a shared apartment, had no outdoor space but was determined to grow his own food. He decided to convert a small closet into a hydroponic garden.

Using deep water culture (DWC), he set up a simple system with a 10-gallon plastic tub, an air pump, and LED grow lights. To improve airflow, he installed a small desk fan and monitored temperature and humidity with a smartphone app. Over three months, John successfully grew lettuce, kale, and even cherry tomatoes.

"The closet garden was a game-changer for me," John says. "It gave me fresh produce, and it was a great conversation starter with my roommates!"

—-

Step 5: Designing Your Layout

Once you've chosen your system, sketch out your layout to ensure everything fits. Keep the following in mind:

Position plants so they all receive adequate light.

Group plants with similar nutrient and water needs.

Leave space for easy access to reservoirs and pumps for maintenance.

—-

Key Takeaways

Evaluate your space carefully to choose a location that meets the needs of your hydroponic system.

Ensure your chosen area has access to light, power, water, and proper ventilation.

Select the right type of hydroponic system based on your space and plant preferences.

Plan your layout to optimize light, airflow, and accessibility.

Now that you've mapped out your hydroponic space, it's time to dive into building your first system. In the next chapter, we'll cover cost-effective DIY systems and step-by-step instructions to get you started.

3

Hydroponic Systems on a Budget

One of the most common misconceptions about hydroponics is that it's expensive or requires specialized equipment. The truth is, you can build a fully functioning hydroponic system with materials you likely already have at home or can purchase inexpensively. In this chapter, we'll explore budget-friendly options for setting up a hydroponic system, provide step-by-step instructions for building your own, and share a success story to inspire your journey.

—-

Why DIY Hydroponics?

Creating your own hydroponic system allows you to:

Save Money: Store-bought systems can be pricey, but DIY setups often cost a fraction of the price.

Customize Your Setup: You can tailor your system to fit your space, budget, and the types of plants you want to grow.

Learn by Doing: Building your system helps you understand how hydroponics works, making troubleshooting easier later on.

Whether you're looking to grow a few herbs or a variety of vegetables, there's a DIY system for you.

—-

Simple DIY Hydroponic Systems

Here are three budget-friendly systems perfect for beginners:

1. Kratky Method

The Kratky method is one of the simplest hydroponic systems. It doesn't require pumps, electricity, or constant monitoring, making it perfect for beginners.

Materials Needed:

A container with a lid (e.g., a plastic storage bin or mason jar)

Net pots (small pots with holes that allow roots to grow through)

Hydroponic nutrient solution

A growing medium (e.g., Rockwool, perlite, or coco coir)

Seeds or seedlings

Drill or knife to cut holes in the lid

Steps:

1. Drill holes in the container's lid to fit the net pots.

2. Fill the container with nutrient solution, ensuring the bottom of the net pots will touch the liquid.

3. Place the seedlings in the growing medium and insert them into the net pots.

4. Cover the container and place it in a well-lit area.

5. Monitor the water level, ensuring the roots stay submerged in the solution as the plants grow.

Estimated Cost: $10–$20.

—-

2. Wick System

The wick system is another simple setup that uses wicks to draw nutrient solution from a reservoir to the plant roots.

Materials Needed:

A container for the reservoir (e.g., a plastic bottle or tub)

Wicks (cotton rope or strips of fabric)

Net pots

Growing medium

Hydroponic nutrient solution

Seeds or seedlings

Steps:

1. Cut holes in the lid of the container to fit the net pots.

2. Thread the wicks through the holes and into the reservoir, ensuring they touch the nutrient solution.

3. Place the seedlings in the growing medium and insert them into the net pots.

4. The wicks will draw nutrient solution to the plant roots as needed.

Estimated Cost: $5–$15.

—-

3. PVC Pipe Hydroponic System

This system is ideal for growing multiple plants in a compact, vertical space. It requires more effort to build but is still affordable.

Materials Needed:

PVC pipes (3–4 inches in diameter)

PVC end caps

A submersible water pump

A plastic tub for the reservoir

Net pots

Growing medium

Hydroponic nutrient solution

Drill and hole saw

Steps:

1. Drill holes in the PVC pipe to fit the net pots, spacing them evenly.

2. Assemble the PVC pipes in a vertical or horizontal layout, sealing the ends with caps.

3. Connect the pipes to a water pump that circulates nutrient solution from the reservoir.

4. Place the seedlings in the growing medium and insert them into the net pots.

5. Run the system, ensuring the water pump evenly distributes the solution.

Estimated Cost: $30–$50.

—-

Tips for Saving Money

Use Recycled Materials: Repurpose old containers, bottles, or tubs to reduce costs.

Buy in Bulk: Purchase nutrient solutions, growing media, and seeds in larger quantities to save money over time.

DIY Accessories: Instead of buying pre-made net pots or wicks, create your own using household items.

—-

Case Study: Emma's Cost-Effective Lettuce Farm

Emma, a student living in a small apartment, wanted to grow her own food but had a limited budget. Using the Kratky method, she built a simple system with a plastic storage bin, net pots, and Rockwool cubes.

Her first attempt yielded fresh basil and lettuce, and she quickly expanded to grow spinach and kale. By investing just $15 in materials, Emma now saves money on groceries and enjoys fresh, pesticide-free greens year-round.

"I was surprised by how easy and affordable it was to get started," Emma shares. "Now, I can't imagine not having my little indoor garden!"

—-

Step-by-Step DIY System: The Kratky Method

Let's walk through building a Kratky system step by step.

Materials Checklist:

A 5-gallon plastic bucket with a lid

3-inch net pots (3–4)

Hydroponic nutrient solution

Rockwool cubes

Seeds

Drill with a 3-inch hole saw

Instructions:

1. Prepare the Bucket:

Drill 3–4 evenly spaced holes in the lid of the bucket to fit the net pots.

2. Mix the Nutrient Solution:

Fill the bucket with water and mix in the hydroponic nutrients according to the package instructions.

3. Set Up the Plants:

Place seeds in Rockwool cubes and let them germinate.

Once the seedlings are established, transfer the cubes to the net pots.

4. Assemble the System:

Insert the net pots into the holes in the lid, ensuring the bottom of the Rockwool touches the nutrient solution.

5. Monitor and Maintain:

Place the bucket in a well-lit area or under a grow light.

Check the water level weekly, refilling with nutrient solution as needed.

Your First Harvest:

Within 4–6 weeks, you'll have fresh lettuce or herbs ready to harvest!

—-

Key Takeaways

Building a hydroponic system on a budget is easier than you think.

Start with simple systems like the Kratky or wick method to gain confidence.

Use affordable or recycled materials to reduce costs further.

Experiment and adapt your setup based on your available space and resources.

In the next chapter, we'll dive into the essentials of plant nutrition and water management, ensuring your plants thrive in your hydroponic system.

4

Nutrients and Water Management

In hydroponics, success hinges on providing plants with the right balance of nutrients and maintaining high-quality water. Unlike traditional gardening, where soil naturally supplies some nutrients, hydroponics relies entirely on you to deliver these essential elements. Don't worry—it's not as complicated as it sounds! This chapter will guide you through the basics of plant nutrition, how to mix nutrient solutions, and the importance of water quality. We'll also explore common challenges and share a real-life example of troubleshooting nutrient issues.

—-

The Role of Nutrients in Hydroponics

Plants require a mix of macronutrients and micronutrients to grow. In soil-based gardening, these nutrients are absorbed from the ground, but in hydroponics, they come directly from a nutrient solution you prepare.

Essential Nutrients for Plants

1. Macronutrients:

Nitrogen (N): Promotes leaf and stem growth.

Phosphorus (P): Supports root development and flowering.

Potassium (K): Helps with overall plant health and disease resistance.

2. Secondary Nutrients:

Calcium (Ca): Strengthens cell walls.

Magnesium (Mg): Vital for photosynthesis.

Sulfur (S): Aids in protein synthesis.

3. Micronutrients: Required in smaller amounts but equally important:

Iron, manganese, zinc, copper, boron, molybdenum, and chlorine.

In hydroponics, all these nutrients are dissolved in water,

creating a solution that plants absorb through their roots.

—-

Mixing Nutrient Solutions

To mix a nutrient solution, you'll need a hydroponic nutrient concentrate. These are available as premixed solutions or powders that you dissolve in water. Here's how to prepare your solution:

Step-by-Step Instructions:

1. Choose the Right Nutrient Solution: Select a formula tailored to your plants. For example, leafy greens like lettuce require higher nitrogen, while fruiting plants like tomatoes need more phosphorus and potassium.

2. Measure Accurately: Follow the manufacturer's instructions to avoid overfeeding or underfeeding your plants. Use a measuring cup or syringe for precision.

3. Check and Adjust pH: Plants absorb nutrients best when the solution has a pH between 5.5 and 6.5. Use a pH meter or test strips to measure, and adjust with pH up or down solutions as needed.

4. Dilute Gradually: Mix the nutrient concentrate with water in your reservoir. Stir thoroughly to ensure even distribution.

5. Monitor the Solution: Regularly test the electrical conductivity (EC) to measure the strength of the solution. Adjust as needed to match your plants' growth stage.

— -

Understanding Water Quality

Water is the backbone of any hydroponic system, and its quality directly impacts your plants. Poor water quality can lead to nutrient imbalances, root damage, and stunted growth.

Key Factors to Monitor:

1. pH Levels: As mentioned, pH affects nutrient absorption. Monitor it weekly and adjust as needed.

2. Hardness: Hard water contains high levels of calcium and magnesium, which can disrupt nutrient balance. If you have hard water, consider using a reverse osmosis (RO) filter.

3. Chlorine: Tap water often contains chlorine or chloramine, which can harm plants. Let tap water sit for 24 hours to allow chlorine to evaporate, or use a water conditioner.

4. Temperature: Water that is too hot or cold can stress plants. Aim for a water temperature of 65–75°F (18–24°C).

—-

Common Challenges and How to Fix Them

Even with the best intentions, issues can arise. Here's how to identify and resolve common problems:

1. Nutrient Deficiencies

Symptoms: Yellowing leaves, stunted growth, or poor flowering.

Solution: Test your nutrient solution's pH and EC levels. Adjust the concentration or add missing nutrients.

2. Algae Growth

Symptoms: Green or slimy growth on water surfaces or system components.

Solution: Reduce light exposure to the nutrient solution by using opaque containers or covering exposed water.

3. Salt Build-Up

Symptoms: White crust on plant roots or containers.

Solution: Flush your system with plain water every few weeks to prevent salt accumulation.

—-

Case Study: Mike's Troubleshooting Journey

Mike, a small business owner with a passion for gardening, decided to grow hydroponic basil in his home office. At first, his plants thrived, but within weeks, the leaves began yellowing, and growth stalled.

After testing the nutrient solution, Mike discovered the pH had dropped below 5.0, preventing his plants from absorbing nutrients. By adjusting the pH with a store-bought solution and monitoring it weekly, Mike restored his basil's health and learned the importance of regular maintenance.

"I thought hydroponics was set-it-and-forget-it, but now I see it's about balance," Mike shares. "It's like learning to ride a bike—once you get it, it's smooth sailing."

—-

Tips for Success

1. Keep a Log: Record your pH, EC, and water changes to track patterns and spot issues early.

2. Start Simple: Begin with a premixed nutrient solution before experimenting with custom formulas.

3. Stay Consistent: Regularly check your system to catch small issues before they become big problems.

4. Use Quality Water: Invest in a water filtration system if your tap water quality is poor.

—-

Key Takeaways

Plants need a balanced mix of macro and micronutrients to thrive in hydroponics.

Preparing and maintaining a nutrient solution involves monitoring pH, EC, and water quality.

Regular testing and adjustments are essential for preventing nutrient deficiencies and other issues.

With proper water management, your hydroponic system will yield healthy, thriving plants.

In the next chapter, we'll explore how to choose the best plants for your hydroponic garden, focusing on those that are beginner-friendly and thrive in small spaces.

5

Choosing the Right Plants for Your Hydroponic Garden

Selecting the right plants for your hydroponic garden is crucial to your success, especially as a beginner. Some plants thrive in hydroponic systems and are more forgiving to novice mistakes, while others can be challenging without experience. In this chapter, we'll explore the best plants for beginners, considerations for advanced growers, and how to plan your garden to maximize growth and yield.

—-

Best Plants for Hydroponics

Certain plants naturally adapt to hydroponic systems due to their growth habits, nutrient requirements, and resilience. Here's a list of beginner-friendly plants to consider for your first garden:

Leafy Greens and Herbs (Ideal for Beginners)

Lettuce: Fast-growing and requires minimal maintenance.

Spinach: Thrives in nutrient-rich water and grows quickly.

Kale: Resilient and perfect for year-round cultivation.

Basil: One of the easiest herbs to grow hydroponically.

Mint: Grows rapidly and fills your system with fresh fragrance.

Cilantro: Great for adding flavor to meals and easy to maintain.

Vegetables (Intermediate)

Tomatoes: Fruit-bearing plants that do well in larger hydroponic setups.

Peppers (Bell and Chili): Need more care but produce bountiful yields.

Cucumbers: Ideal for vertical systems; grow quickly and produce high yields.

Fruits (Advanced)

Strawberries: Require specific care but thrive in systems like the NFT.

Melons: Challenging due to space needs but rewarding for experienced growers.

—-

Factors to Consider When Choosing Plants

When deciding what to grow, keep the following factors in mind:

1. Space Requirements:

Leafy greens like lettuce require little space, while fruiting plants like tomatoes need more room to spread.

Consider vertical systems for space efficiency if growing vining plants like cucumbers.

2. Growth Speed:

For quick results, start with fast-growing plants like lettuce or spinach. These are perfect for learning the basics of hydroponics.

3. Light Needs:

Some plants, like basil and tomatoes, need more light to thrive. If you're relying on natural light, choose plants that match your space's light availability.

4. System Compatibility:

Compact plants (lettuce, herbs) work well in simple systems like the Kratky method.

Larger plants (tomatoes, peppers) perform better in advanced systems like deep water culture (DWC) or nutrient film technique (NFT).

5. Climate and Environment:

Leafy greens prefer cooler temperatures, while fruiting plants like peppers thrive in warmer conditions. Tailor your plant choices to your local climate or indoor setup.

—-

Planning Your Garden

Before you start planting, map out your garden layout. This ensures efficient use of space and helps prevent overcrowding, which can lead to competition for nutrients and light.

Tips for Effective Planning:

Group Plants by Growth Rate: Pair fast-growing plants like

lettuce with others that have similar timelines to avoid competition.

Consider Root Space: Some plants, like kale, have deeper root systems and require more room in the reservoir.

Stagger Planting Times: For continuous harvests, plant new seeds every 2–3 weeks.

—-

Starting with Seeds or Seedlings

You can grow plants in hydroponics either by starting from seeds or transplanting seedlings. Each approach has its benefits:

Seeds:

Cost-effective and widely available.

Allow full control over the growing process.

Seedlings:

Save time, as the initial germination phase is already complete.

Ideal for plants that are harder to germinate, like peppers.

—-

Step-by-Step Guide to Starting Seeds

1. Choose a Growing Medium: Rockwool cubes, coco coir, or perlite are excellent options.

2. Soak the Medium: Wet the growing medium with water and place it in a tray or container.

3. Plant Seeds: Place 1–2 seeds in each growing medium and lightly cover.

4. Provide Warmth and Moisture: Keep the seeds in a warm, humid environment (65–75°F) until they germinate.

5. Transfer to the System: Once the seedlings have a few leaves and roots, move them to your hydroponic system.

—-

Case Study: Ravi's Success with Strawberries

Ravi, a graphic designer with a small patio, wanted to grow strawberries for his family. After researching, he built a vertical hydroponic system using PVC pipes. Although strawberries are considered challenging for beginners, Ravi followed these steps for success:

Chose a nutrient film technique (NFT) system for even water distribution.

Used seedlings to bypass the germination phase.

Monitored pH and nutrient levels diligently, maintaining a pH of 5.8–6.2.

Within three months, Ravi's system was producing sweet, juicy strawberries. "The effort was worth it," Ravi shares. "Now I'm inspired to expand my garden to include peppers and lettuce."

— -

Advanced Tips for Experienced Growers

Once you're comfortable with basic plants, challenge yourself with more complex crops:

Use Trellises: For vining plants like cucumbers or tomatoes, trellises can support vertical growth.

Experiment with Companion Planting: Pair plants that complement each other, such as basil and tomatoes, to improve yields and deter pests.

Try Custom Nutrient Blends: Tailor nutrient solutions to the specific needs of advanced crops like strawberries or melons.

—-

Key Takeaways

Start with beginner-friendly plants like lettuce, spinach, and herbs.

Choose plants that match your system, space, and light availability.

Plan your garden layout to maximize space and ensure plants receive adequate nutrients and light.

Start with seeds or seedlings depending on your preference and experience level.

As you gain confidence, experiment with more complex crops and advanced techniques.

In the next chapter, we'll delve into lighting your hydroponic garden, including tips for natural sunlight and how to choose and use grow lights effectively.

6

Lighting Your Garden: Sunlight vs. Artificial Lights

Light is the lifeblood of any garden, and in hydroponics, ensuring your plants receive enough light is essential for healthy growth. Whether you're using natural sunlight or artificial grow lights, the right lighting setup will directly impact the success of your hydroponic system. In this chapter, we'll explore how plants use light, the benefits and challenges of different lighting options, and how to create the perfect lighting conditions for your garden.

—-

How Plants Use Light

Light powers photosynthesis, the process through which plants convert light, carbon dioxide, and water into energy. To grow successfully, plants need light in the right intensity, duration, and spectrum.

Light Spectrum:

Blue Light (400–500 nm): Promotes vegetative growth (leaves and stems).

Red Light (600–700 nm): Encourages flowering and fruiting.

Full Spectrum: Most plants need a combination of blue and red light for optimal growth.

—-

Natural Sunlight for Hydroponics

For those with access to ample natural light, sunlight can be an effective and cost-free option. However, natural light has limitations, particularly in urban settings or during winter months.

Benefits of Sunlight:

Free and abundant (in the right conditions).

Provides the full spectrum of light needed for plant growth.

No additional equipment or energy costs.

Challenges of Sunlight:

Light intensity varies throughout the day and seasons.

Windows and urban environments can block or filter light.

Not all spaces have sufficient exposure to direct sunlight.

Tips for Maximizing Sunlight:

1. Choose South-Facing Windows: In the northern hemisphere, south-facing windows receive the most sunlight.

2. Rotate Plants: Ensure all sides of the plant receive equal light exposure to prevent uneven growth.

3. Supplement When Needed: Use artificial lights during cloudy days or shorter winter days.

— -

Artificial Grow Lights

Artificial grow lights offer control and consistency, making them a popular choice for indoor hydroponic gardens. They can be tailored to provide the specific light spectrum and intensity your plants need, regardless of natural light availability.

Types of Grow Lights:

1. LED Grow Lights:

Energy-efficient, long-lasting, and customizable to different light spectrums.

Emit very little heat, making them safe for indoor use.

Ideal for beginners and advanced growers alike.

2. Fluorescent Lights (CFLs and T5s):

Affordable and widely available.

Best for small setups or starting seedlings.

Less efficient and powerful than LEDs.

3. High-Intensity Discharge (HID) Lights:

Provide intense light suitable for larger systems.

Include Metal Halide (MH) lights for vegetative growth and High-Pressure Sodium (HPS) lights for flowering.

Require additional equipment like ballasts and cooling systems.

—-

Choosing the Right Grow Lights

The type of grow light you choose will depend on your space, budget, and the plants you're growing.

Factors to Consider:

1. Light Intensity: Fruiting plants like tomatoes need high-intensity light, while leafy greens like lettuce require less.

2. Coverage Area: Ensure the light covers all plants in your system evenly.

3. Energy Efficiency: LEDs are the most cost-effective option in the long run due to their low energy consumption and longevity.

4. Heat Output: Avoid overheating your plants by choosing lights with low heat emissions or using a cooling system.

— -

Setting Up Your Lighting System

Once you've chosen your grow lights, proper setup is key to ensuring your plants thrive.

1. Positioning:

Keep the lights 12–18 inches above your plants for most LED and fluorescent lights.

Adjust the height as plants grow to maintain consistent light intensity.

2. Light Duration:

Most plants need 12–16 hours of light per day. Use a timer to automate the lighting schedule.

Provide a period of darkness (6–8 hours) to allow plants to rest.

3. Reflective Surfaces:

Use reflective materials like aluminum foil or Mylar to maximize light distribution and reduce energy waste.

4. Monitoring:

Regularly check plants for signs of insufficient or excessive light:

Too little light: Leggy, weak stems and pale leaves.

Too much light: Leaf burn, curling, or discoloration.

—-

Case Study: Lisa's Studio Apartment Garden

Lisa, a graphic designer living in a small studio apartment, wanted to grow her own herbs and vegetables. With no access to natural sunlight, she invested in LED grow lights and set up a simple Kratky hydroponic system on a shelf near her desk.

Lisa chose a full-spectrum LED panel and used a timer to provide her plants with 16 hours of light daily. Within weeks, her lettuce and basil were thriving. "The grow lights made all the difference," Lisa says. "It was like having a little slice of nature indoors."

Her success inspired her to expand her system to include cherry tomatoes. By using a trellis and adjusting her lights for the taller plants, Lisa created a productive indoor garden in just a few square feet.

—-

Advanced Tips for Optimizing Light

1. Invest in a PAR Meter: Measure the Photosynthetically Active Radiation (PAR) to ensure your plants receive the right light intensity.

2. Experiment with Light Spectrums: Some LEDs allow you to adjust the spectrum for different growth stages.

3. Avoid Overheating: Use fans or ventilation to keep your garden cool and prevent heat stress.

— -

Key Takeaways

Light is essential for photosynthesis and healthy plant growth in hydroponics.

Natural sunlight is free but may need supplementation in urban or indoor environments.

Artificial grow lights provide control and consistency, with LEDs being the most efficient choice.

Proper setup, including positioning, duration, and reflective surfaces, ensures optimal plant growth.

Regularly monitor your plants to adjust light conditions as needed.

In the next chapter, we'll focus on maintaining your hydroponic garden, covering essential tasks like cleaning, monitoring, and troubleshooting common issues to ensure long-term success.

7

Maintaining Your Hydroponic Garden

Setting up your hydroponic garden is an exciting first step, but maintaining it ensures long-term success. While hydroponics requires less labor than traditional gardening, regular upkeep is essential to keep your plants healthy and productive. In this chapter, we'll explore essential maintenance tasks, common challenges, and best practices for monitoring and troubleshooting your system. By the end of this chapter, you'll be equipped with the tools to keep your garden thriving.

—-

Daily Maintenance

Hydroponic systems require consistent attention to function properly. Here are the daily tasks you should incorporate into your routine:

1. Check Water Levels

Plants in hydroponic systems rely entirely on the nutrient solution, so maintaining an adequate water level is critical.

Ensure the roots remain submerged in the solution or in contact with it.

Add water as needed to compensate for evaporation and plant uptake.

2. Monitor Plant Health

Inspect your plants for signs of stress, such as:

Yellowing Leaves: May indicate a nutrient deficiency or pH imbalance.

Wilting: Could be due to low water levels or poor aeration.

Pest Damage: Look for holes, spots, or visible insects.

3. Ensure Proper Light Exposure

Verify that your grow lights are functioning and positioned correctly.

Adjust the height of the lights as your plants grow to avoid burning the leaves.

—-

Weekly Maintenance

In addition to daily checks, dedicate time each week for deeper inspections and adjustments.

1. Test and Adjust pH Levels

pH is one of the most important factors in hydroponic gardening. Plants absorb nutrients most effectively within a pH range of 5.5 to 6.5.

Use a pH meter or test strips to check your solution.

Adjust the pH using a pH up or pH down solution as needed.

2. Replenish Nutrient Solution

As plants consume nutrients, the concentration in the solution decreases.

Check the electrical conductivity (EC) or total dissolved solids (TDS) to measure nutrient levels.

Refill the reservoir with a fresh nutrient solution according to the manufacturer's instructions.

3. Inspect System Components

Ensure pumps, tubing, and other equipment are functioning

properly.

Clean any debris or buildup from the system to maintain efficiency.

— -

Monthly Maintenance

Monthly maintenance focuses on deep cleaning and system optimization.

1. Clean the Reservoir

Over time, algae and mineral deposits can accumulate in the reservoir, affecting water quality.

Empty the reservoir completely and scrub it with a mild cleaning solution (e.g., white vinegar and water).

Rinse thoroughly before refilling.

2. Prune Plants

Remove dead or yellowing leaves to prevent mold and improve airflow. For vining plants, trim excess growth to keep them manageable and productive.

3. Inspect Roots

Healthy roots are white or light tan and firm to the touch.

If roots appear brown or slimy, it could indicate root rot caused by poor aeration or pathogens. Address this by increasing oxygen levels or treating with a hydroponic-safe fungicide.

—-

Troubleshooting Common Issues

Even with proper maintenance, challenges can arise. Here's how to identify and resolve common problems:

1. Algae Growth

Symptoms: Green slime or film on water surfaces or equipment.

Solution: Reduce light exposure by covering reservoirs with opaque materials. Clean affected surfaces regularly.

2. Nutrient Imbalances

Symptoms: Stunted growth, yellowing leaves, or other abnormal plant behavior.

Solution: Test nutrient levels and adjust the solution accordingly. Flush the system if necessary to reset the balance.

3. Pests

Symptoms: Holes in leaves, sticky residue, or visible insects like aphids or spider mites.

Solution: Use neem oil or insecticidal soap to control pests. Maintain a clean growing environment to prevent infestations.

4. System Failures

Symptoms: Pump malfunctions, clogged tubing, or inconsistent water flow.

Solution: Regularly inspect and clean all components. Keep spare parts on hand for quick repairs.

—-

Preventative Maintenance Tips

Preventing problems before they occur saves time and effort in the long run. Here are some proactive steps you can take:

Use High-Quality Materials: Invest in reliable pumps, tubing, and grow lights to minimize breakdowns.

Control Humidity: Maintain humidity levels between 40% and 70% to reduce the risk of mold and mildew.

Rotate Crops: If growing the same plants repeatedly, sanitize the system between crops to prevent disease buildup.

—-

Case Study: Mark's Recovery from a Mold Infestation

Mark, a marketing professional with a passion for gardening, noticed a white mold growing on his kale plants a few months into his hydroponic journey. He initially panicked, fearing his entire crop was lost.

Mark took the following steps to recover:

1. Removed Affected Plants: He discarded heavily infected plants to prevent the spread of mold.

2. Sanitized the System: Mark deep-cleaned his entire setup, including the reservoir, tubing, and growing trays, with a hydrogen peroxide solution.

3. Improved Airflow: He added a small fan to increase ventilation and reduce humidity.

4. Monitored Daily: For the next two weeks, Mark inspected his plants closely and adjusted his setup as needed.

Thanks to his quick action and diligent maintenance, Mark salvaged most of his crop and avoided future infestations. "It was a learning experience," he says. "Now I'm more proactive, and my system runs better than ever."

—-

Key Takeaways

Regular maintenance is essential to keep your hydroponic system running smoothly.

Daily, weekly, and monthly tasks ensure plants receive the care they need.

Monitoring water levels, pH, and nutrient concentrations helps prevent common problems.

Proactive measures like cleaning, pruning, and inspecting equipment reduce the risk of system failures and plant issues.

In the next chapter, we'll explore how to expand your hydroponic garden, including scaling up your system, growing new crops, and optimizing space for higher yields.

8

Scaling Up: Expanding Your Hydroponic Garden

Once you've mastered the basics of hydroponic gardening, the next step is scaling up your system to grow more plants, try new crops, or increase your yields. Expanding your garden can be both rewarding and challenging, but with proper planning, you can create a larger system that remains efficient, manageable, and productive. In this chapter, we'll explore the benefits of scaling up, the different types of expansion, and how to optimize your system for growth.

—-

Why Scale Up Your Garden?

Expanding your hydroponic garden offers several advantages:

1. Increased Yield: Grow more produce to feed your household or even sell at local markets.

2. Crop Variety: Experiment with new plants or grow different crops simultaneously.

3. Maximized Space: Make the most of unused areas in your home, balcony, or backyard.

4. Skill Development: Build on your knowledge and challenge yourself with more complex systems.

Whether you're looking to grow additional plants or take on advanced techniques, scaling up allows you to make the most of your hydroponic setup.

— -

Types of Expansion

1. Adding More Plants

If you have space in your current system, you can simply increase the number of plants. This is the easiest way to expand without significant changes.

Example: Adding more net pots to an unused section of your deep water culture (DWC) reservoir.

2. Building a New System

Creating a second system allows you to experiment with different crops, growing methods, or system designs.

Example: Keeping your existing Kratky system for herbs while building an ebb-and-flow system for fruiting vegetables like peppers.

3. Creating a Vertical Garden

Vertical systems are ideal for maximizing limited space. By growing upward instead of outward, you can cultivate a larger number of plants in the same footprint.

Example: Using PVC pipes or tiered shelves to grow lettuce, strawberries, or herbs.

4. Expanding with Automation

Scaling up often requires more effort, but automation can reduce your workload. Adding timers, sensors, or automated pumps ensures your system stays efficient as it grows.

Planning for Expansion

Before expanding, take time to plan your new setup. Consider the following factors:

1. Space and Layout

Evaluate the available area and choose a design that fits comfortably.

Ensure proper access to light, water, and power for all plants.

2. Plant Selection

Group plants with similar light, nutrient, and water requirements.

Avoid overcrowding by allowing enough space for each plant's growth.

3. System Type

Choose a system that matches your goals and available resources.

For small expansions: Wick or Kratky systems.

For larger setups: Nutrient film technique (NFT) or aeroponics.

4. Budget

Account for the costs of additional materials, nutrient solution, and energy use.

Look for ways to save by repurposing items or buying materials in bulk.

—-

Step-by-Step Guide: Building a Vertical Hydroponic System

One of the most efficient ways to expand your garden is by creating a vertical hydroponic system. Here's how to get started:

Materials Needed:

PVC pipes (3–4 inches in diameter)

Net pots

Submersible water pump

Plastic reservoir (e.g., a large tote or bucket)

Tubing for water circulation

Drill and hole saw

Timer for the pump

Hydroponic nutrient solution

Instructions:

1. Prepare the PVC Pipes:

Drill evenly spaced holes to fit the net pots.

Arrange the pipes vertically or in a slight incline for proper water flow.

2. Assemble the System:

Connect the pipes to the reservoir using tubing.

Install the submersible pump in the reservoir to circulate the nutrient solution.

3. Set Up the Plants:

Fill the net pots with your chosen growing medium (e.g., Rockwool or perlite).

Place seedlings in the net pots and insert them into the pipe openings.

4. Test the System:

Run the pump to ensure the nutrient solution flows evenly through the system.

Adjust the pump's timer to provide regular intervals of nutrient delivery.

5. Optimize Light:

Position grow lights above the system or near a sunny window.

— -

Optimizing Your Expanded Garden

As your garden grows, maintaining efficiency becomes crucial. Here are some tips to optimize your setup:

1. Manage Nutrient Levels

Larger systems consume more nutrients, so monitor your reservoir closely and replenish the solution regularly. Consider investing in a larger reservoir to reduce the frequency of refills.

2. Balance Light Exposure

Ensure all plants receive adequate light, especially in vertical setups. Reflective surfaces or additional grow lights can help distribute light evenly.

3. Improve Airflow

Prevent mold and pests by increasing airflow with fans or ventilation systems. This is especially important in tightly packed gardens.

4. Use Automation

Timers and sensors can help automate watering, lighting, and nutrient delivery, reducing manual effort as your system scales.

—-

Case Study: Anna's Vertical Garden

Anna, a school teacher with limited outdoor space, decided to expand her hydroponic garden to grow more food for her family. Using a vertical PVC pipe system, she transformed a corner of her balcony into a thriving garden.

Steps Anna Took:

1. Built a vertical NFT system using recycled PVC pipes and a 20-gallon reservoir.

2. Installed an LED grow light panel to supplement sunlight.

3. Used a timer to automate the water pump, ensuring consistent

nutrient delivery.

Within two months, Anna's vertical garden was producing enough lettuce, spinach, and strawberries to reduce her grocery bill significantly. "Scaling up was intimidating at first," Anna says, "but now I feel like a hydroponics pro!"

—-

Advanced Scaling: Starting a Community Garden

If you're ready to take your passion for hydroponics to the next level, consider starting a community garden. Sharing resources and expertise with neighbors can lead to larger, collaborative systems that benefit everyone.

Steps to Start a Community Garden:

1. Find a suitable location, such as a rooftop, school, or community center.

2. Recruit participants and pool resources for materials and equipment.

3. Choose crops that cater to the group's needs and preferences.

4. Educate participants on maintenance tasks and system care.

— -

Key Takeaways

Scaling up your hydroponic garden allows you to grow more plants, try new crops, and maximize your space.

Options for expansion include adding plants, building new systems, or creating vertical gardens.

Proper planning ensures your expanded setup remains efficient and manageable.

Automation and optimization techniques reduce the workload as your garden grows.

Larger systems can foster community collaboration, turning your passion into a shared endeavor.

In the next chapter, we'll focus on troubleshooting advanced issues, equipping you with the skills to handle challenges in a larger hydroponic setup.

9

Troubleshooting Advanced Issues in Hydroponic Gardening

As your hydroponic garden grows in size and complexity, new challenges may arise. Even the most experienced hydroponic gardeners encounter issues, but with the right knowledge and tools, you can address them effectively. This chapter will help you identify and resolve advanced problems related to nutrient imbalances, equipment failures, environmental factors, and plant health.

—-

Common Advanced Issues in Hydroponic Gardening

1. Nutrient Imbalances

As your garden expands, maintaining the right nutrient balance becomes more challenging. An imbalance can lead to poor plant health and reduced yields.

Symptoms:

Nitrogen Deficiency: Yellowing of older leaves, stunted growth.

Phosphorus Deficiency: Dark green or purplish leaves, poor flowering.

Potassium Deficiency: Yellow or brown edges on leaves.

Solutions:

1. Test Nutrient Levels: Use an EC (electrical conductivity) meter to monitor the strength of your solution. High readings indicate excessive nutrients, while low readings signal deficiencies.

2. Adjust Concentrations: Add more nutrients if the levels are low or dilute the solution with water if the levels are too high.

3. Flush the System: Periodically rinse your system with plain water to prevent salt buildup.

—-

2. Equipment Failures

With more components in a larger system, the chances of equipment failure increase. Pumps, timers, and grow lights are the most common culprits.

Symptoms:

Inconsistent water flow.

Lights flickering or not turning on.

Pumps making unusual noises or not working.

Solutions:

1. Inspect Regularly: Check all components weekly for signs of wear or malfunction.

2. Keep Spares: Have extra pumps, bulbs, and tubing on hand for quick replacements.

3. Invest in Quality Equipment: Durable, reliable tools reduce the likelihood of failure.

— -

3. Root Problems

In larger systems, roots can become tangled, oxygen-deprived, or infected.

Symptoms:

Slimy, brown roots (root rot).

Foul odor in the reservoir.

Stunted growth despite proper nutrient levels.

Solutions:

1. Increase Oxygenation: Use additional air stones or larger pumps to aerate the water.

2. Control Water Temperature: Keep the reservoir temperature between 65–75°F (18–24°C) to prevent pathogen growth.

3. Treat Infections: Apply a hydroponic-safe fungicide or beneficial microbes to combat root rot.

— -

4. Pest Infestations

Even in indoor setups, pests can infiltrate your garden, especially as you grow more plants.

Symptoms:

Visible insects (e.g., aphids, spider mites).

Sticky residue on leaves (honeydew from pests).

Webbing or small holes on plants.

Solutions:

1. Identify the Pest: Use a magnifying glass to confirm the type of pest and choose the appropriate treatment.

2. Apply Natural Remedies: Neem oil, insecticidal soap, or predatory insects (like ladybugs) can control infestations without harming plants.

3. Maintain Cleanliness: Regularly clean your system and remove dead leaves or debris.

— -

5. Algae Growth

Algae thrive in nutrient-rich water exposed to light, especially in larger systems with multiple reservoirs.

Symptoms:

Green or brown slime on surfaces or in the reservoir.

Clogged tubing or reduced water flow.

Solutions:

1. Block Light: Cover reservoirs and tubing with opaque materials to prevent light penetration.

2. Clean Regularly: Scrub algae from surfaces using a mild solution of hydrogen peroxide and water.

3. Add Beneficial Organisms: Introduce algae-eating fish or snails in aquaponic systems.

—-

Environmental Challenges

1. Temperature Extremes

Larger systems may be harder to maintain at stable temperatures, especially in fluctuating climates.

Solutions:

Use heaters or chillers to regulate water temperature.

Insulate reservoirs to minimize temperature fluctuations.

Monitor the growing area with a thermometer and adjust as needed.

2. Humidity Control

High humidity can lead to mold and fungal issues, while low humidity may stress plants.

Solutions:

Install a dehumidifier in high-humidity environments.

Use a humidifier in dry conditions.

Increase airflow with fans to maintain consistent humidity levels.

— -

Advanced Monitoring Tools

To stay ahead of potential issues, consider investing in advanced monitoring tools:

1. pH and EC Meters:

Measure the acidity and nutrient strength of your solution.

Look for digital meters with automatic calibration for accuracy.

2. Environmental Sensors:

Monitor temperature, humidity, and CO2 levels in your growing area.

Some systems sync with smartphones for real-time alerts.

3. Cameras:

Set up cameras to observe your garden remotely, ensuring plants and equipment are functioning correctly.

—-

Case Study: Tom's Battle with Root Rot

Tom, an engineer with a passion for hydroponics, expanded his garden to include a nutrient film technique (NFT) system for strawberries. A month into his expansion, he noticed his plants wilting despite maintaining proper nutrient levels.

After inspecting the roots, Tom discovered they were brown and slimy—a clear sign of root rot. He immediately took the following steps:

1. Flushed the System: Tom drained the reservoir, cleaned all components with hydrogen peroxide, and refilled it with fresh nutrient solution.

2. Increased Aeration: He added extra air stones to the reservoir to boost oxygen levels.

3. Controlled Temperature: Tom installed a water chiller to keep the reservoir temperature below 70°F (21°C).

Within weeks, his plants recovered, and he avoided further root rot by monitoring oxygen levels and water temperature consistently.

— -

Tips for Preventative Maintenance

Regular Cleaning: Schedule deep cleans for your system every 4–6 weeks.

Create a Maintenance Log: Record pH, EC, temperature, and other metrics to identify patterns or potential issues.

Monitor Closely After Changes: When adding new plants or components, watch your system carefully for signs of stress or imbalance.

Start Small with Expansions: Test changes on a smaller scale before implementing them across your entire garden.

— -

Key Takeaways

Advanced issues like nutrient imbalances, root problems, and equipment failures require close monitoring and timely action.

Proper oxygenation, temperature control, and regular cleaning prevent common problems.

Invest in monitoring tools to identify and address issues before they escalate.

Case studies like Tom's show that even significant challenges can be overcome with the right steps.

In the next chapter, we'll explore the future of hydroponics and how it can play a role in sustainable urban living, including tips on sharing your produce, teaching others, and even starting a small hydroponic business.

10

The Future of Hydroponics and Sustainable Urban Living

As cities grow and green spaces shrink, hydroponics offers a powerful solution for sustainable urban living. Beyond its potential to provide fresh, local produce, hydroponics can address environmental challenges, foster community connections, and even open doors to new opportunities. In this final chapter, we'll explore how hydroponics fits into the future of urban agriculture, discuss ways to share your knowledge and produce, and provide tips for scaling your passion into a business or community project.

—-

Hydroponics and Sustainability

Hydroponics is inherently more sustainable than traditional agriculture. Here's why:

1. Water Conservation

Hydroponic systems use up to 90% less water than soil-based farming by recirculating water and nutrients. This makes it a viable solution for regions facing water scarcity.

2. Reduced Land Use

Hydroponics eliminates the need for large plots of land, making it perfect for urban environments. Vertical systems can further optimize space, allowing growers to produce more in less room.

3. Lower Carbon Footprint

Growing your own food reduces the environmental impact of transporting produce over long distances. Hydroponics also minimizes the use of harmful pesticides and fertilizers that can pollute soil and water.

4. Year-Round Growing

With hydroponics, you can cultivate fresh produce regardless of season, ensuring a consistent food supply and reducing dependency on imports.

—-

Sharing Your Harvest and Knowledge

As your hydroponic garden thrives, consider ways to share the benefits with others. Here are some ideas:

1. Share Your Produce

Donate excess produce to local food banks or shelters.

Offer fresh vegetables and herbs to friends, family, or neighbors.

Start a small market stand or join a community-supported agriculture (CSA) program.

2. Educate Others

Host workshops or demonstrations to teach hydroponic gardening.

Share your journey on social media or a blog, providing tips and insights.

Partner with local schools to introduce students to sustainable agriculture.

3. Build a Community Garden

Bring neighbors together by creating a shared hydroponic space in a community center, rooftop, or vacant lot. This fosters collaboration and provides fresh produce for everyone involved.

—-

Turning Your Passion Into a Business

If you're ready to take your hydroponic gardening to the next level, consider turning it into a business. Here are some ideas to get started:

1. Selling Produce

Focus on high-value crops like basil, microgreens, or strawberries.

Supply local restaurants, cafes, or farmers' markets with fresh, pesticide-free produce.

Market your produce as sustainable and locally grown to attract eco-conscious customers.

2. Designing Systems for Others

Build and install hydroponic systems for individuals, schools, or businesses.

Offer maintenance services or training for those new to hydroponics.

3. Creating DIY Kits

Package affordable hydroponic kits for beginners, complete with instructions, materials, and seeds.

Sell online or at gardening stores to reach a broader audience.

4. Consulting

Offer your expertise to organizations looking to implement hydroponic systems, such as urban farms or educational institutions.

Hydroponics in Urban Agriculture

Hydroponics is a key component of urban agriculture, which seeks to integrate food production into cities. Innovations in this field include:

1. Rooftop Farms

Large hydroponic setups on rooftops can transform underutilized spaces into productive food sources. Cities like New York and Tokyo are already embracing this concept.

2. Vertical Farming

Indoor vertical farms use hydroponics and LED lighting to produce food on a large scale. These systems can feed urban populations while minimizing environmental impact.

3. Aquaponics

Combining hydroponics with aquaculture (fish farming) creates a closed-loop system where fish waste provides nutrients for plants, and plants filter water for the fish.

—-

Case Study: Maya's Hydroponic Community Garden

Maya, a software developer and avid gardener, started her hydroponic journey with a small Kratky system in her kitchen. Inspired by her success, she expanded to a vertical garden on her balcony. Seeing the potential to help others, Maya partnered with a local community center to create a shared hydroponic garden.

Steps Maya Took:

1. Secured Funding: She applied for a local sustainability grant to cover materials and equipment.

2. Built the Garden: Maya and volunteers installed several vertical systems in the community center courtyard.

3. Educated Participants: She hosted workshops to teach participants how to maintain the garden and use the produce.

4. Expanded Outreach: Maya worked with local schools to involve students in hydroponics, turning the garden into a hands-on learning space.

Today, the garden provides fresh produce for dozens of families while educating the next generation about sustainable agriculture. "Hydroponics brought our community together," Maya says. "It's about more than just growing food—it's about growing connections."

—-

The Future of Hydroponics

Hydroponics has the potential to revolutionize how we grow and consume food. As technology advances, expect to see innovations such as:

Automated Systems: AI-powered sensors and apps to monitor and optimize growing conditions.

Energy Efficiency: Solar-powered hydroponic systems to reduce reliance on traditional energy sources.

Urban Integration: Hydroponic gardens becoming a standard feature in urban architecture, such as green walls and indoor farms.

By adopting hydroponics, individuals and communities can contribute to a more sustainable and resilient food system.

—-

Key Takeaways

Hydroponics plays a crucial role in sustainable urban living by conserving resources, reducing waste, and producing fresh food year-round.

Sharing your produce and knowledge can inspire others and foster community connections.

Scaling your hydroponic garden into a business or community project opens doors to new opportunities.

The future of hydroponics is bright, with innovations poised to transform urban agriculture.

As you conclude this book, remember that hydroponics is a journey. Whether you're growing for yourself, your community, or the planet, your efforts contribute to a greener, more sustainable future. Keep experimenting, learning, and sharing your passion for hydroponic gardening.